ROCKET AROUND
Switzerland

Neurodiverse-friendly activity + coloring book

Written by
Lee Lynch

Illustrations
Emma Lynch

Contributors
Jeffrey, Jack, & Tom Lynch

Guest Appearance
Dottie

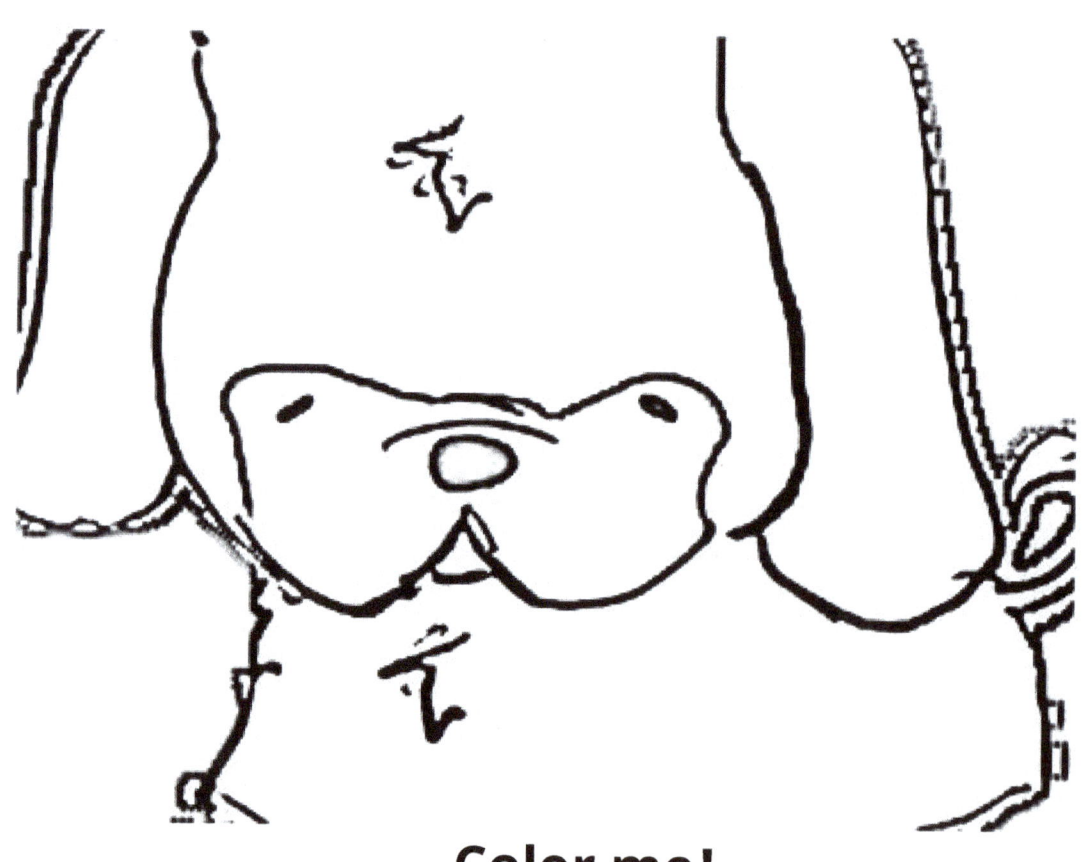

Color me!

ROCKET AROUND LLC

TABLE OF CONTENTS

Neurodiverse SUPERpowers

In Switzerland or where you live, neurodiverse people behave, think, and learn differently from people with neurotypical brains. Neurodiverse people might be autistic, live with ADHD, dyslexia, PTSD, Tourette's, or other things. Their differences include strengths. In a word, neurodiverse people are awesome.

What are your superpowers?
Write them below!

1. _____
2. _____
3. _____
4. _____
5. _____
6. _____
7. _____
8. _____
9. _____
10. _____

You're
SUPER!

A few examples of neurodiverse superpowers:

Creativity
Focus
Paying attention to detail
Caring about others
Curiosity
Solving problems
Asking great questions
Good memory
Remembering details
Fast thinking
Lots of energy
Good with numbers
Good with pictures
Doing puzzles

Safety Matters

What are 5 things you can do to stay safe when you're on an adventure to Switzerland or anywhere else? Write them here!

1._____

2. _____

3. _____

4. _____

5. _____

Turn over to see possible answers

- Make sure you can see the human you're with
- Set a meeting place in case you cannot find your human
- Know your human's phone number - write it here: _____
- Wear a brightly colored shirt
- If you feel lost, ask a police officer or information human for help

Don't Get on the Plane Without It

What are 5 things you want to bring on your plane trip? Write them here!

1._____

2. _____

3. _____

4. _____

5. _____

Examples of things to bring on an adventure to Switzerland

- A backpack
- Water bottle
- Healthy snacks
- Fidgets
- Tissues
- Devices to keep in touch
- Headphones
- Paper, pencil, crayons
- Card game
- Sweatshirt or coat
- Money
- The phone number of the human you're with
- Your passport
- *Rocket Around Switzerland Visual Guide and Activity Book*!

Fun Facts about Switzerland

Draw a line from the fact on the left to the correct answer on the right.
(Answers on next page)

Facts

The water fountain (Jet d'Eau) in this city shoots water 125 miles per hour!

6,500 flowers and bushes are used to create the face of this in Geneva.

This yummy cheese dish is the national dish of Switzerland.

This staircase made a path between two markets of Lausanne's old city.

Located in Lausanne, this is the largest freshwater aquarium in Europe.

Answers

Market staircase

Aquatis

Flower Clock

Fondue

Geneva

ANSWERS to Fun Facts about Switzerland

Facts

The water fountain (Jet d'Eau) in this city shoots water 125 miles per hour!

6,500 flowers and bushes are used to create the face of this in Geneva.

This yummy cheese dish is the national dish of Switzerland.

This staircase made a path between two markets of Lausanne's old city.

Located in Lausanne, this is the largest freshwater aquarium in Europe.

Answers

Market staircase

Aquatis

Flower Clock

Fondue

Geneva

GREAT Work!

More Fun Facts about Switzerland

Draw a line from the fact on the left to the correct answers on the right.
(Answers on next page)

Facts

This Lausanne museum has about 1,500 objects from different Olympics.

These mountains stretch across 65 percent of Switzerland.

A long wooden horn that helped people living in the Alps communicate.

Switzerland has 3,000+ miles of this, all running on electricity.

Switzerland's largest city.

Answers

Alpine horn (or alphorn)

The Alps

Zurich

The Olympic Museum

Railway

ANSWERS to More Fun Facts

Facts

This Lausanne museum has about 1,500 objects from different Olympics.

These mountains stretch across [65 percent of Switzerland](#).

A long wooden horn that helped people living in the Alps communicate.

Switzerland has 3,000+ miles of this, all running on electricity.

Switzerland's largest city.

Answers

Alpine horn (or [alphorn](#))

The [Alps](#)

Zurich

The Olympic Museum

Railway

Way to GO!

Switzerland Word Search #1

Alps   Chapel   Geneva   Lake

Bridge   Cheese   Harbor   Lake

Burgenstock   Chocolate

Look left-to-right and up-to-down for the words above

```
S Q Q C O J K L H H A S Z Q R O C K E T
S N W H I B D C J Y R U E W D U Z H A W
T L E O K O E D O C H E E S E Z O V R G
O B F C J F P E B F R N S Z J R A Z J I
L N K O T M O X M Y X F S Z I Y H M E Y
N U W L H A R B O R T S M O U N T A I N
X J L A L P G T M W R R E E F L E K B B
Y Z I T W H X U O D A X F A D A N Z C C
C D M E V F H O D O I R F B K K Q K X B
R H M P T B W L J U N R N T K E L Z J P
P W A O Z U R I C H U G E N E V A L R J
P B T L M O V G D B O L O R W G U B N G
L D P B S L Z R Q A B A O I L L S N E Q
A N Z I S R A T Q D R K V P I L A T U S
N P F F R J O W A J J E X M Y Y N C U X
E A S R N X F Q N U E C F F O X N V C U
E S C K F B R I D G E L O L U C E R N E
M T L F H P W I X V Z M R B V Y H K Q I
S W I T Z E R L A N D X U O A L P S P ⁷
B U R G E N S T O C K C H A P E L G U
```

10

ANSWERS for Word Search #1

Alps   Chapel   Geneva   Lake

Bridge   Cheese   Harbor   Lake

Burgenstock   Chocolate

```
S Q Q C O J K L H H A S Z Q R O C K E T
S N W H I B D C J Y R U E W D U Z H A W
T L E O K O E D O C H E E S E Z O V R G
O B F C J F P E B F R N S Z J R A Z J I
L N K O T M O X M Y X F S Z I Y H M E Y
N U W L H A R B O R T S M O U N T A I N
X J L A L P G T M W R R E E F L E K B B
Y Z I T W H X U O D A X F A D A N Z C C
C D M E V F H O D O I R F B K K Q K X B
R H M P T B W L J U N R N T K E L Z J P
P W A O Z U R I C H U G E N E V A L R J
P B T L M O V G D B O L O R W G U B N G
L D P B S L Z R Q A B A O I L L S N E Q
A N Z I S R A T Q D R K V P I L A T U S
N P F F R J O W A J J E X M Y Y N C U X
E A S R N X F Q N U E C F F O X N V C U
E S C K F B R I D G E L O L U C E R N E
M T L F H P W I X V Z M R B V Y H K Q I
S W I T Z E R L A N D X U O A L P S P Z
B U R G E N S T O C K C H A P E L G U Y
```

11

Switzerland Word Search #2

Lausanne   Mountain   Rocket   Train
Limmat   Pilatus   Switzerland   Zurich
Lucerne   Plane

Look left-to-right and up-to-down for the words above

```
S Q Q C O J K L H H A S Z Q R O C K E T
S N W H I B D C J Y R U E W D U Z H A W
T L E O K O E D O C H E E S E Z O V R G
O B F C J F P E B F R N S Z J R A Z J I
L N K O T M O X M Y X F S Z I Y H M E Y
N U W L H A R B O R T S M O U N T A I N
X J L A L P G T M W R R E E F L E K B B
Y Z I T W H X U O D A X F A D A N Z C C
C D M E V F H O D O I R F B K K Q K X B
R H M P T B W L J U N R N T K E L Z J P
P W A O Z U R I C H U G E N E V A L R J
P B T L M O V G D B O L O R W G U B N G
L D P B S L Z R Q A B A O I L L S N E Q
A N Z I S R A T Q D R K V P I L A T U S
N P F F R J O W A J J E X M Y Y N C U X
E A S R N X F Q N U E C F F O X N V C U
E S C K F B R I D G E L O L U C E R N E
M T L F H P W I X V Z M R B V Y H K Q I
S W I T Z E R L A N D X U O A L P S P
B U R G E N S T O C K C H A P E L G U 12
```

ANSWERS for Word Search #2

Lausanne   Mountain   Rocket   Train
Limmat   Pilatus   Switzerland   Zurich
Lucerne   Plane

```
S Q Q C O J K L H H A S Z Q R O C K E T
S N W H I B D C J Y R U E W D U Z H A W
T L E O K O E D O C H E E S E Z O V R G
O B F C J F P E B F R N S Z J R A Z J I
L N K O T M O X M Y X F S Z I Y H M E Y
N U W L H A R B O R T S M O U N T A I N
X J L A L P G T M W R R E E F L E K B B
Y Z I T W H X U O D A X F A D A N Z C C
C D M E V F H O D O I R F B K K Q K X B
R H M P T B W L J U N R N T K E L Z J P
P W A O Z U R I C H U G E N E V A L R J
P B T L M O V G D B O L O R W G U B N G
L D P B S L Z R Q A B A O I L L S N E Q
A N Z I S R A T Q D R K V P I L A T U S
N P F F R J O W A J J E X M Y Y N C U X
E A S R N X F Q N U E C F F O X N V C U
E S C K F B R I D G E L O L U C E R N E
M T L F H P W I X V Z M R B V Y H K Q I
S W I T Z E R L A N D X U O A L P S P Z
B U R G E N S T O C K C H A P E L G U Y
```

13

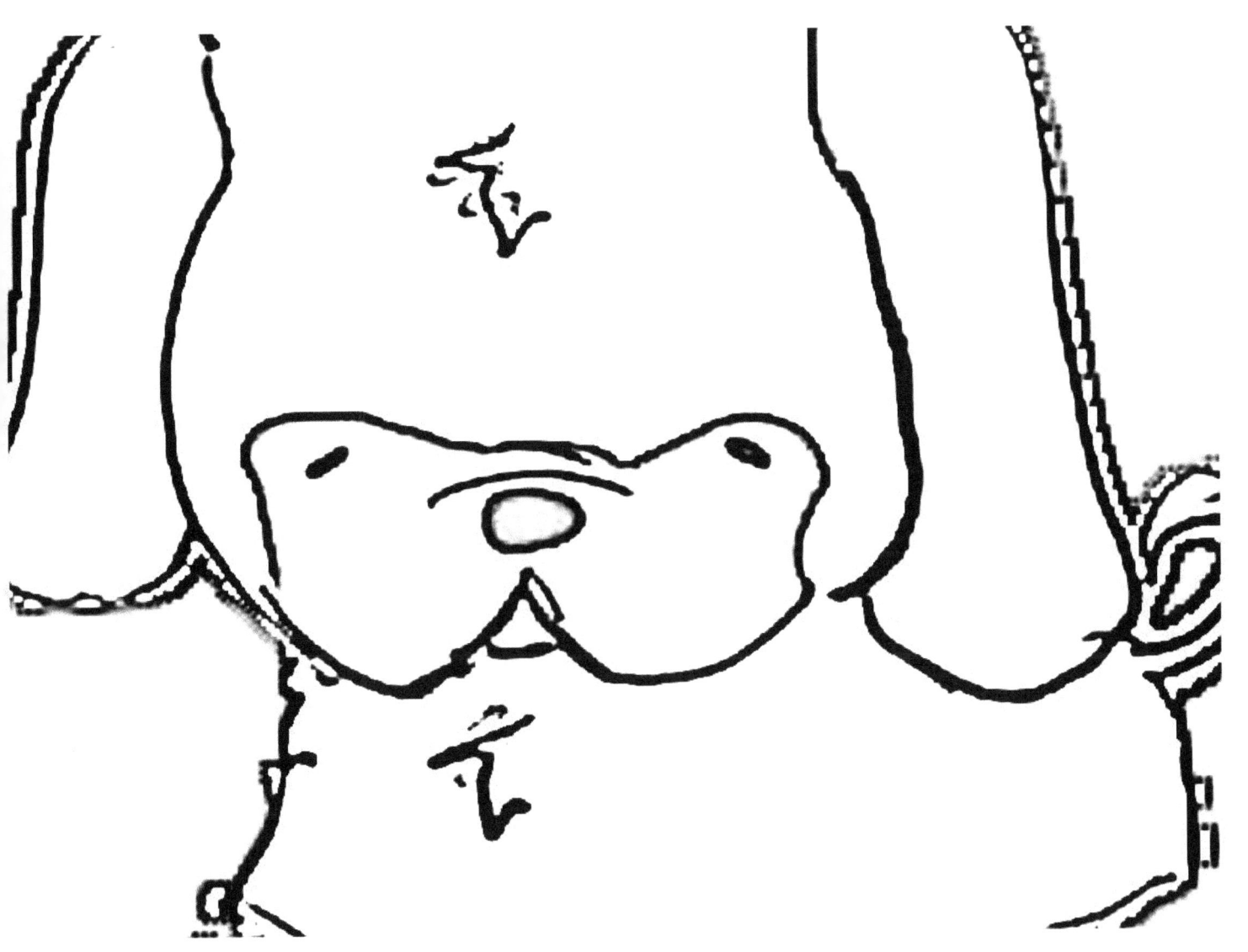

Switzerland Pattern Play

Look at the position of each of the sites in the boxes below. Which sites would continue the pattern? See the answers on the next page.

ANSWERS Switzerland Pattern Play

Switzerland Sites

Write the name of each memorial or monument next to each picture

Write the names below next to pictures at left (see answers on the next page):

Mount Pilatus in the Swiss Alps

Grand-Pont bridge in Lausanne

Old Town Lucerne

Chapel Bridge in Lucerne

Swiss Museum of Transport

Limmat River in Zurich

Switzerland Sites ANSWERS

Grand-Pont

Limmat River

Old Town Lucerne

Mount Pilatus

Chapel Bridge

Swiss Museum of Transport

~~Mount Pilatus in the Swiss Alps~~

~~Grand-Pont bridge in Lausanne~~

~~Old Town Lucerne~~

~~Chapel Bridge in Lucerne~~

~~Swiss Museum of Transport~~

~~Limmat River in Zurich~~

German Phrase Matching Game

German is the most widely spoken language in Switzerland.

Match the correct English and German phrases. ANSWERS on next page.

English	**German**
Hello	Wie sagst du das auf Englisch
How are you today?	Hallo
My name is	Kannst du mir helfen
Can you help me	Auf Wiedersehen!
Where is	Wie geht es dir heute
I am lost	Wie heissen Sie
I love to rocket around	Ich bin verloren
How do you say in English?	Wo ist
Good bye!	Ich liebe es, durch die Gegend zu rasen

ANSWERS for German Phrase Matching Game

English	German
Hello	Wie sagst du das auf Englisch
How are you today?	Hallo
My name is	Kannst du mir helfen
Can you help me	Auf Wiedersehen!
Where is	Wie geht es dir heute
I am lost	Wie heissen Sie
I love to rocket around	Ich bin verloren
How do you say in English?	Wo ist
Good bye!	Ich liebe es, durch die Gegend zu rasen

French Phrase Matching Game

French is spoken in the "Suisse Romande" – the western part of Switzerland.

Match the correct English and French phrases. ANSWERS on next page.

English	**French**
Hello	Comment dites-vous en anglais
How are you today?	Pouvez-vous m'aider
My name is	J'aime faire des fusées
What is your name?	Bonjour
Can you help me	Comment allez-vous aujourd'hui
Where is	Je suis perdu
I am lost	Quel est ton nom
I love to rocket around	Mon nom est
How do you say in English?	Où est
Good bye!	Au revoir!

ANSWERS for the French Phrase Matching Game

English	French
English	**French**

Hello

How are you today?

My name is

What is your name?

Can you help me

Where is

I am lost

I love to rocket around

How do you say in English?

Good bye!

Comment dites-vous en anglais

Pouvez-vous m'aider

J'aime faire des fusées

Bonjour

Comment allez-vous aujourd'hui

Je suis perdu

Quel est ton nom

Mon nom est

Où est

Au revoir!

Switzerland By the Numbers

See the answers on the next page

Which of the numbers on the right match the facts below? Write them below

The water jet fountain in Geneva shoots up _____ feet

Number of miles of railway in Switzerland _____

Spreuer Bridge has more than _____ paintings on the ceiling

The Chapel in the middle of Chapel Bridge is about _____ years old

The Olympic Museum has about _____ objects from different Olympics

The Alps stretch across _____ percent of Switzerland

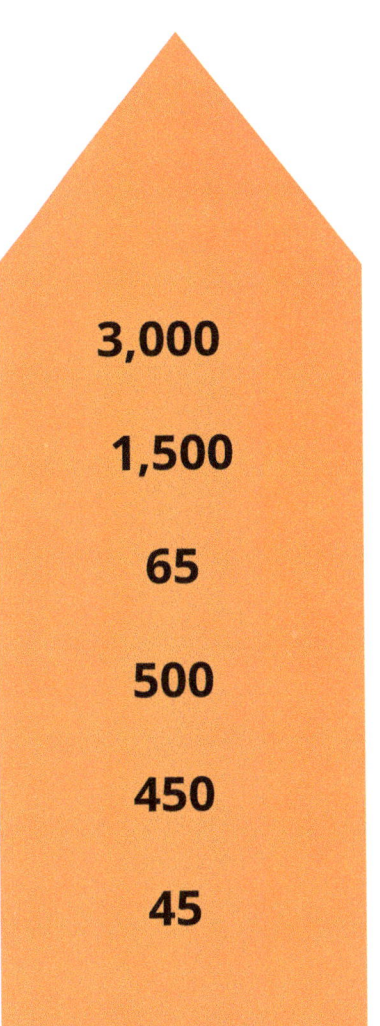

3,000

1,500

65

500

450

45

ANSWERS for Switzerland By the Numbers

The water jet fountain in Geneva shoots up
____450____feet

Number of miles of railway in Switzerland
____3000____

Spreuer Bridge has more than ____45____ paintings on the ceiling

The Chapel in the middle of Chapel Bridge is about ___500_____ years old

The Olympic Museum has about
____1500____ objects from different Olympics

The Alps stretch across ____65____ percent of Switzerland

You're SUPER!

3,000

1,500

65

500

450

45

Transportation test

Which of these different kinds of transportation do you think is faster?

Pedal car at the Swiss Transport Museum vs. an air gondola?

*Write your
answer here:*

_____

Air gondola vs. Swiss train?

*Write your
answer here:*

_____

Swiss train vs. Rocket rocketing around?

*Write your
answer here:*

_____

Drawing Time - Rocket and Dottie

Here's a picture of Rocket and Dottie. Now you draw it below the line.

· ·

GREAT job!

What in the WORD?!

Write words in the blanks below. Read the story to your favorite human.

(The following is from pages 26 to 28 of *Rocket Around Switzerland - A neurodiverse-friendly storybook*)

Hey look - it's another pup - a _____.
They come from the Swiss _____. She'll
know her way around here!

Wait, my humans are LEAVING? Come on Dottie - my
humans are heading back across _____
and I hear them saying they are going to
_____ – let's go, we won't want to miss
that! What a trip - my humans took a bus, then walked up a
big hill to an _____ (which is like
_____) and now are on a bigger
_____. Whoa, we just broke through
the _____!

Mount Pilatus is right in front of us, and the Alps - the
longest _____ in all of
_____ – and the countryside is all around us!

Map of Switzerland

Match the numbers to the sites on the next page. Color the map!

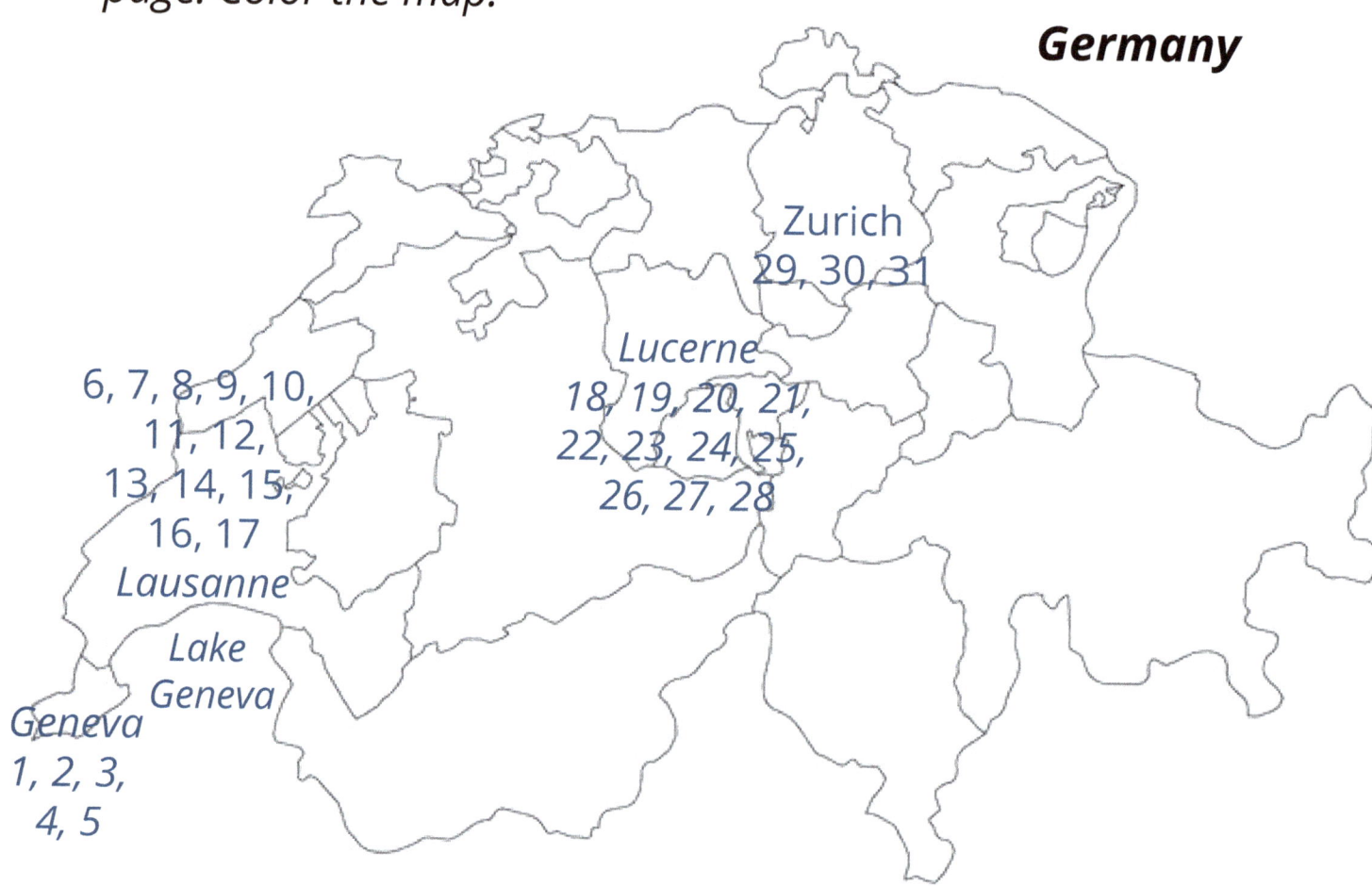

Germany

Zurich
29, 30, 31

6, 7, 8, 9, 10,
11, 12,
13, 14, 15,
16, 17
Lausanne

Lucerne
18, 19, 20, 21,
22, 23, 24, 25,
26, 27, 28

Lake
Geneva

Geneva
1, 2, 3,
4, 5

What's on The Map

Geneva:
1. Water jet fountain
2. Flower Clock English Garden park
3. Exploracentre science center
4. Natural History Museum
5. International Museum of the Red Cross and Red Crescent

Lausanne:
6. Ouchy Promenade
7. Old Harbor
8. Olympic Museum
9. Cathedrale de Lausanne
10. Cite hill
11. Market staircase
12. Restaurant with fondue
13. Place de la Palud
14. Lausanne City Hall
15. Fountain of Justice
16. Grand-Pont
17. Church of Saint Francois

Lucerne:
18. Old Town Lucerne
19. River Reuss
20. Lake Lucerne
21. Mount Burgenstock
22. Mount Pilatus
23. Mill Square
24. Spreuer Bridge
25. Chapel Bridge
26. Swiss Museum of Transport
27. Port of Lucerne
28. Swiss Alps

Zurich:
29. Lake Zürich
30. Limmat river
31. Chocolate Fountain

Scavenger Hunt

Find the pictures of the things below on the pages of this book (look on all pages) or find them in Switzerland.

See answers on the next page.

1. Rocket in a backpack
2. Safety tips
3. Rocket and Dottie feeling cold
4. A picture of a church on Mount Pilatus
5. Colorful house in Old Town Lucerne
6. The German phrase for "Can you help me?"
7. The French phrase for "Good bye!"
8. A red air gondola
9. A picture of purple flowers in Geneva
10. A picture of the Grand-Pont bridge
11. A map of Switzerland
12. A picture of Emma on a swing

ANSWERS for Scavenger Hunt

1. Rocket in a backpack - pages 5, 38, and 40
2. Safety tips - page 4
3. Rocket and Dottie feeling cold, page 16
4. A picture of a church on Mount Pilatus, pages 18, 19, 20, 21
5. Colorful house in Old Town Lucerne, pages 18, 19, 20, and 21
6. The German phrase for "Can you help me?", pages 22 and 23
7. The French phrase for "Good bye!", pages 24 and 25
8. A red air gondola, pages 28, and 35
9. A picture of purple flowers in Geneva, page 35
10. A picture of the Grand-Pont bridge, pages 20, 21, and 35
11. A map of Switzerland, page 29
12. A picture of Emma on a swing, pages 35

Great job!

Rocket Around Switzerland Game Board

See directions on the next page and HAVE FUN!

FINISH!

START

Rocket Around Switzerland Board Game Directions

The goal of the game is to get from the START to the FINISH first using your board game piece. Here's how to play:

1. Cut out the board game character and number pieces on the next page.
2. Each player chooses a board game character piece.
3. Fold each character piece at the word FOLD and put each piece at the START square on the board game.
4. Cut out the board game number pieces on the next page. Put each number face down in the middle of the board game.
5. Each player picks a number - the person with the highest number goes first. If a player gets a Back 1 or Skip turn piece, draw again.
6. Put the numbers face down again in the middle of the board. Keep choosing numbers until each player's position to start is determined.
7. To start, put the numbers face down again in the middle of the board. The first player will choose a number, move that many spaces on the board, put their number face down again in the middle of the board, and shuffle the numbers around.
8. When it's a new player's turn, they will choose a number, move that many spaces on the board, put their number face down again in the middle of the board, and shuffle the numbers around.
9. Continue to move in the same order by picking a game number piece until someone reaches the FINISH square and WINS!
10. When you're done, put the game pieces in the back pocket of this book.

HAVE FUN!

Board Game Pieces

*Cut out the board game pieces below to play
the Rocket Around Switzerland Board Game*

Board Game Character Pieces

Rocket
backpack
(FOLD)

Dottie
(FOLD)

Sneaky
Rocket
(FOLD)

Rocket
Flight
Attendant
(FOLD)

Sleeping
Rocket
(FOLD)

Board Game Number Pieces

1	1	1	1	Back 1	Skip turn
2	2	2	3	3	4

EXTRA Board Game Pieces

Cut out the board game pieces below to play the Rocket Around Switzerland Board Game

Board Game Character Pieces

Rocket backpack (FOLD)

Dottie (FOLD)

Sneaky Rocket (FOLD)

Rocket Flight Attendant (FOLD)

Sleeping Rocket (FOLD)

Board Game Number Pieces

1   1   1   1   Back 1   Skip turn

2   2   2   3   3   4

Storage Pocket for Board Game Pieces

How to use this page:

- *Cut it out along the dotted line.*
- *Tape or staple sides 1, 2, and 3 of this page on the inside of the back cover of this book.*
- *Do not tape or staple side 4 - it needs to remain open.*
- *Slide the board pieces from the previous page into the open side 4 and store your board game pieces there when you are not using them.*

Be a Rocketarounder!

--Do the activities in *Rocket Around Switzerland - Neurodiverse-friendly activity + coloring book*.

-- Look for more activities on rocketaround.com to build your brain with Rocket!

--Let Rocket's human family know: Where should Rocket and his humans go next? Where would your dog want to rocket around with Rocket? (make sure your mom and dad are okay with it first). Email your ideas to lee@rocketaround.com

If you did these things, GREAT JOB! You are an official Rocketarounder - welcome to the Club!

I'M A ROCKETAROUNDER!
I build my brain through:
-Adventure
-Imagination
-Finding new ways to have fun!

Rocket Around Switzerland - Neurodiverse-friendly activity + coloring book

More from Rocket Around

Books:

Rocket Around Washington DC – a neurodiverse-friendly visual guide with activities

Rocket Around Washington DC – a neurodiverse-friendly storybook

Rocket Around Washington DC! Neurodiverse activity + coloring book

Rocket Around Washington DC Ebook

Rocket Around Switzerland - Neurodiverse-friendly visual guide + activities

Rocket Around Switzerland - Neurodiverse-friendly storybook

Rocket Around Switzerland! Neurodiverse-friendly activity + coloring book

On the Internet:

Rocketaround.com blogsite on adventure & life for neuodiverse families

Facebook - https://www.facebook.com/groups/rocketaround

Instagram - https://instagram.com/rocketaroundtheglobe?igshid=YmMyMTA2M2Y=)

Pinterest - https://www.pinterest.com/rocketaround/

Look for other Rocket Around books and kids' activities at rocketaround.com!